DATE DUE

DEMCO 38-297

Ferdinand Magellan

by Ruth Harley
illustrated by Hal Frenck

Troll Associates

Troll Associates, Mahwah, N.J.
Library of Congress Catalog Card Number: 78-18058
ISBN 0-89375-176-6
ISBN 0-89375-168-5 Paper Edition

Ferdinand Magellan

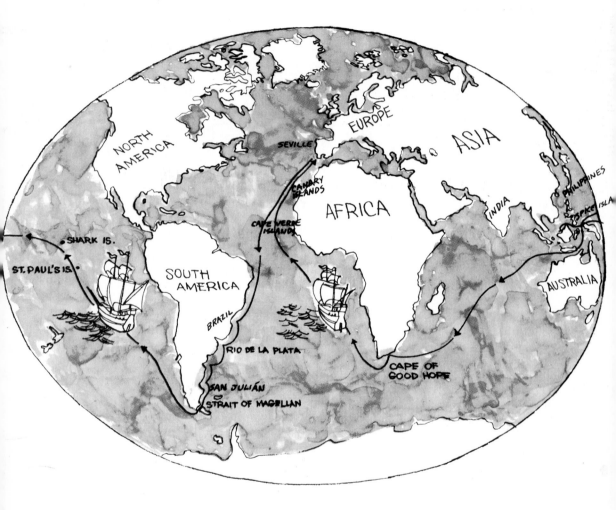

NORTH AMERICA

EUROPE

ASIA

SEVILLE

CANARY ISLANDS

AFRICA

INDIA

PHILIPPINES

SPICE ISLA

SHARK IS.

ST. PAUL'S IS.

CAPE VERDE ISLANDS

SOUTH AMERICA

BRAZIL

AUSTRALIA

RIO DE LA PLATA

CAPE OF GOOD HOPE

SAN JULIÁN

STRAIT OF MAGELLAN

Upstairs in the stone farmhouse where he lived, young Ferdinand Magellan knew he should be sleeping. But his dark brown eyes were wide open. Tomorrow he would start school at the monastery. He wondered what school would be like.

Ferdinand could hear the cattle moving around below. Many years ago, the building had been a fort. Now the Magellan family lived upstairs. The farm animals lived on the ground floor.

Ferdinand's father was a Portuguese nobleman. He owned a large amount of land in northern Portugal. It was there that Ferdinand was born about 1480.

5

It turned out that Ferdinand liked school. The monks taught him Latin and arithmetic. He was a good student. When he was 12, he was made a page in the court of Queen Leonor. His brother, Diogo, and his cousin, Francisco Serrano, were also pages for the queen.

Pages in the royal court received a good education. When the three boys were not running errands or acting as ushers, they were taking lessons in music and dancing, and learning about riding and handling weapons. The queen's brother Manuel was in charge of teaching the pages astronomy, mapmaking, and navigation. Manuel was ten years older than Ferdinand, and the two did not like each other at all. Nevertheless, Ferdinand worked hard, because he wanted to be a navigator.

As a page, Ferdinand could see all the famous visitors who came to court. One day in 1493, Christopher Columbus stopped to pay his respects to King John. Columbus was on his way home to Spain from the New World.

6

The voyage of Columbus had caused a real conflict between Spain and Portugal. Both countries were now claiming the same territories. There was danger of war.

In 1494, a conference was held in Spain to settle the matter. The globe was divided into two parts. Portugal was to keep the eastern half of the world. Portugal could have any new lands discovered there. Spain was to have the western half, which included the Americas, and the Pacific Ocean— then called the "Sea of the South." The Dividing Line ran north and south, about 550 miles west of Portugal's Cape Verde Islands.

Many educated people believed the world was round, but no one in Europe knew what was on the other side of it. How far was it from America to Asia? Could a ship actually sail around the world?

In 1495, when King John died, Manuel became king of Portugal. Things changed for the three young pages, too. Ferdinand, Diogo, and Francisco were transferred to the king's maritime service. They were put to work in the government trading company called the India House.

The three boys were working there when the explorer Vasco da Gama came back from the famous voyage that took him south around the continent of Africa to India. His success was very important to the spice trade.

The dull food of the Europeans tasted much better when it was seasoned with pepper, cinnamon, nutmeg, ginger, or cloves. All these products came from plants that grew in India, Ceylon, Sumatra, and the Spice Islands in Indonesia.

Spice merchants bought the fragrant dried leaves, seeds, and bark quite cheaply. Then they sold them for a hundred times as much in the markets of Europe. Spice merchants could become very rich. But it was difficult to get the products from the East to Europe. The shipments had to change hands many times. Part of the trip had to be made over land—across the hot deserts of Africa. But then Vasco da Gama proved that the entire trip could be made by water! Ferdinand spent many hours dreaming of making this very voyage some day.

11

In 1502, King Manuel sent Vasco da Gama on a
new trip to India. The work of outfitting his ships
was assigned to the India House, where Ferdinand,
Diogo, and Francisco were working.

12

Even though Portuguese ships were busy and
tradesmen were becoming wealthy, young noblemen in the king's trading company were poorly
paid. Already in his early twenties, Ferdinand
Magellan had no desire to spend his entire life in
the dusty warehouses of the India House. He was a
trained soldier and a navigator. He had spent
enough time outfitting others to go on voyages.
Now he wanted to go himself!

At last, in 1505, the three young men were sent on an important expedition. Its purpose was to capture port cities in India and Africa for the use of Portuguese trading ships. For the next four years, Ferdinand, Diogo, and Francisco led adventurous lives. They helped sail the ships at sea—and fought as soldiers on land.

In 1509, Ferdinand Magellan took part in a bloody battle to win the Malayan island of Malacca for Portugal. He risked his life to save his cousin Francisco Serrano from death at the hands of Malayan warriors. The Portuguese failed to win Malacca. They had to sail away—but they planned to return.

Two years later, Magellan was ready to sail home to Portugal. During his years in India, he had collected a large amount of pepper. If he could sell the pepper in Portugal, he would be a rich man. But 100 miles away from India, his ship ran aground and the bags of pepper were lost!

Now, his fortune gone, Magellan saw no reason to go back to Portugal. So he returned to India, where he continued to serve the Portuguese governor.

17

A few months later, when the governor decided to lead an expedition to try once again to capture Malacca, Magellan was given command of one of the fleet's 19 ships. This time the Portuguese were successful. After a long battle, Malacca was theirs!

Several months after the battle, Magellan secretly explored the area, sailing as far east as the Philippine Islands.

Then one day Magellan decided to sail for Portugal. He was now a veteran of over seven years of warfare in India, Africa, and the Orient. But he was still a poor man. Other men had made fortunes from the rich spice trade he had helped to build. When Magellan finally returned to Lisbon, he was made a gentleman-in-waiting to King Manuel. After all his years of service, he was still little more than a servant.

When Malacca had been won, Magellan's cousin Francisco had gone to the Spice Islands. He liked it there so much that he stayed. It wasn't long before he became a wealthy trader. Serrano wrote often to his cousin. "Come and live here—this is your chance to become rich!"

18

Magellan still had his dreams. He wanted an increase in pay and the rank that went with it. Most of all, he wanted to get to the Spice Islands, where Serrano was living. A plan had begun to form in his mind. He would ask the king for permission to lead a fleet eastward to the Spice Islands and capture them for Portugal. He knew he could do it.

He wrote a letter to the king asking for a private audience. But no answer came. Impatient for action, he joined the Portuguese army that was being sent to fight the Moors in North Africa. In one battle there, he was wounded so badly in the knee that he limped for the rest of his life.

When he returned to Portugal, Magellan asked once more to see King Manuel. Again, weeks went by, and no answer came.

At last, Magellan could no longer stand the suspense. On a day when citizens were allowed to see the king without an appointment, he limped forward into the great throne room as the members of the court watched. First, he asked the king for an increase in pay. The king refused.

Next, Magellan asked to be put in command of a royal ship to sail to the Spice Islands. "I will capture these rich islands for you, Sire!" Again the king said no. He even refused to let Magellan go to the islands on a private ship.

Now Magellan was frustrated and angry. "Then," he asked, "does your Royal Highness object if I enter the service of another lord?"

The king's answer was that he did not care *where* Magellan went or *what* he did! Then, as Magellan was kneeling to kiss Manuel's ring, the king turned his back. Stunned, Magellan rose and hobbled from the hall. Jeers from the onlookers rang in his ears.

Magellan had been publicly disgraced, but he was not defeated. He would get to the Spice Islands another way. Secretly, he began to study the maps in the royal chartroom. He found a map that showed a *strait*—a water passage—through South America. If he could not sail east to the Spice Islands, maybe he could find a western route—under the flag of Spain.

24

Soon the opportunity that Magellan had been waiting for came to him. When he had served the governor of India in 1511, he had become a close friend of Duarte Barbosa, a young Spanish scholar who shared Magellan's interest in geography. Barbosa told him that his wealthy father was now searching for an experienced captain to lead an expedition west across the Atlantic to the Spice Islands.

Late in October 1517, Magellan secretly traveled to Spain. In Seville, a new chapter in his life began. He was treated with respect by the Spaniards.

Now his dreams were within reach. But before he could organize an expedition, he had to get the approval of the king of Spain, 17-year-old Charles I. Magellan rehearsed what he would say to the young king. He took along a small globe of the world on which he had painted the route he would take. Magellan told the king that he believed the Spice Islands lay within the Spanish half of the world. And he said he was convinced that he could find a waterway through South America. He even read aloud the letters from Francisco Serrano describing the riches of the Spice Islands. This was just what the king wanted to hear!

The king liked Magellan. He agreed to provide and equip five ships. Magellan would have a share in any profits. If more than six new islands were discovered, Magellan could have part ownership in two of them. The contract was signed on March 22, 1518.

Magellan worked quickly to get his expedition
under way. He supervised the repair of the five old
ships that had been bought for him. He ordered
supplies for two years at sea. He hired 270 men—
from nine different countries—for the crews.

But things were not as smooth as they seemed. Wealthy Spanish noblemen had lent the king money for Magellan's expedition. These men insisted that three of the ships be commanded by Spanish captains. From the beginning, the three captains plotted against Magellan. Later, at sea, they planned to get rid of him. Then they could claim the riches of the Spice Islands for themselves.

When Manuel of Portugal learned of the expedition, he tried to bribe Magellan to come back home. Magellan refused. Manuel sent secret agents to try to keep Magellan from succeeding. He wanted the Spice Islands for *his* country!

At last, the five ships were anchored in the river at Seville for the final loading. The *Trinidad*, the *San Antonio*, the *Concepción*, the *Victoria*, and the *Santiago* glistened in the sun. Their masts had been scraped and oiled. Their sides were painted yellow and trimmed with black. A great red and gold signal lantern swung to and fro on Magellan's flagship, the *Trinidad*.

The ships were a splendid sight, but aboard them were only a few men Magellan could trust. One was his friend, Duarte Barbosa. Another was Juan Serrano, Francisco's brother. He was captain of the *Santiago*. And sailing on Magellan's flagship was young Antonio Pigafetta from Italy. He kept a careful day-by-day account of the famous voyage.

On September 20, 1519, the ships set sail from southern Spain. They stopped first at the Canary Islands. There, a fast ship from Spain overtook them. Magellan received a secret message from Diogo Barbosa, who had found out about the plot of the three Spanish captains. "Be careful," the message said. "These men mean to kill you!"

When he sailed from the Canary Islands, Magellan deliberately steered east of the route he had charted. As a result, the five ships spent twenty hot, humid days near the equator in the dreaded calm that sailors call the *doldrums*. The captains complained, but Magellan remained silent and grim. He had changed his course to escape an attack from Portuguese ships he knew were lying in wait for him farther west.

When Magellan's ships reached Brazil on December 8, the friendly South Americans supplied them with fowl, pigs, sweet potatoes, and pineapples. Then, after two weeks, the ships headed south along the coast of South America.

On January 11, 1520, the fleet came to a wide inlet. At first, Magellan thought it was the passage he was seeking, but it proved to be the mouth of the Plata River. He confidently told his men that the real passage through the continent was only a little farther south. The ships sailed on. Each opening in the coastline was searched—but without success.

32

By March, hail and snow were falling. The rigging and sails were frozen stiff. Howling winds blew night and day. At last, Magellan called a halt. The ships would spend the winter months—from March to August in the Southern Hemisphere—in the harbor they called Port San Julián. He cut the daily rations so that the food would last longer.

The Spanish captains tried to mutiny and take over the expedition. They were aided by many of the Spanish crewmen, who disliked sailing under a Portuguese leader. But Magellan swiftly restored order. One captain was killed during the mutiny, and a second was sentenced to death. A Spanish nobleman who had been a leader of the mutiny was left on the coast of South America when the ships sailed on. Later, Magellan pardoned about forty of the mutineers, including Sebastian del Cano, who was a good pilot. Magellan knew he would need him.

During the winter months, the men built huts on shore. They made warm clothing for themselves from the skins of seals. Magellan sent the *Santiago* to sail the coast farther south in search of a passage. But near the mouth of the Santa Cruz, a strong wind caught the ship and swept it onto the beach. Only one man was killed, but the *Santiago* would never sail again.

Word had spread among the native South Americans that there were strange men at San Julián. Tribespeople gathered to stare at the sailors and their ships. The South Americans seemed like giants to the Europeans. "Our heads," wrote Pigafetta, "came only to their waists." Magellan named them Big Feet.

In October, when the weather improved, Magellan gave orders for sailing. His officers objected. Again, they wanted to give up the search for the strait and sail to the Spice Islands. Magellan persuaded them to head south. But when they reached a bay that looked promising, the officers did not want to explore it.

Sternly, Magellan ordered the *San Antonio* and the *Concepción* to sail westward into the dark bay. The *Trinidad* and the *Victoria* were to explore the northern and southern shores.

Suddenly, a fierce storm came up and separated the fleet. Magellan feared that the other three ships were lost. Instead, the storm drove the *San Antonio* and *Concepción* far into the bay. Now their captains sighted an opening on the other side. It was the passage to the "Sea of the South."

The two ships came racing back in triumph—sails billowing, flags flying. The men fired cannons in celebration and danced and cheered. Tears of joy flowed from the stern captain's eyes. Magellan offered a prayer of thanksgiving. At last, they had reached the strait that today bears Ferdinand Magellan's name.

Magellan held a meeting with his officers. Many wanted to mark the newly discovered strait on their charts and then leave it, sailing back to Spain in triumph. But Magellan vowed they would go on—even if they had to eat the leather on the ship's rigging. He was determined to keep his promise to the king and sail westward to the Spice Islands. "God will take care of us for the completion of the voyage," Magellan told the men.

The ships separated again to search for the best channel. The men aboard the *Trinidad* found the right passage, but only three ships returned to the meeting place. The *San Antonio* had been seized by mutineers. It was already sailing back to Spain. With the *San Antonio* went more than a third of the fleet's food and supplies.

On November 28, 1520, the remaining ships sailed into the ocean that the explorer Vasco de Balboa had seen from the Isthmus of Panama in 1513. Magellan named it the Pacific Ocean because it seemed so calm.

The little fleet headed west. Like toy boats on the broad Pacific, they sailed for 98 days under the blazing sun.

The food soon ran out. The sailors ate dry biscuits that were crawling with worms. The water was yellow and foul-tasting. The men even ate sawdust, and caught and cooked the rats on the ship.

Sick and discouraged, the crewmen often fought with each other. Nineteen died. Thirty others were so sick with scurvy that they could do nothing. And Magellan's vow to eat the leather from the rigging actually came true.

On January 24, 1521, the men sighted a barren little island. It had little to offer in the way of food. The sailors found crabs and a few nests of turtle eggs. On February 4, they sighted another island. From their ships, they could see palm trees heavy with coconuts. But there was no place for them to drop anchor in the deep water. They had to sail on.

Now the suffering was terrible. The exhausted men no longer tried to raise or lower the sails. They just sailed west, night and day. The Pacific Ocean was far, far wider than anyone had imagined. Some of the men feared that it was endless. Through it all, Magellan was calm. He personally cared for his sick and dying men.

On the evening of March 5, a young lookout thought he spied land. Darkness fell before he could be sure. At dawn, he again struggled up the rigging to the crow's nest. He tried to call out, but his throat was too dry. At last he cried, "Praise God! Praise God! Land! Land! Land!" They had reached Guam in the Mariana Islands.

For the first time in weeks, the sailors had fresh fruit and vegetables to eat.

On March 16, the ships reached the islands later called the Philippines. In 1512, Magellan had sailed east from Malacca and reached these same islands. Now he knew that he had almost *circumnavigated*—completely circled—the globe. He could claim the Philippines for Spain because they lay on the Spanish side of the Dividing Line.

The fresh food gave the men strength, and their spirits were raised by the success of their trip. There was joy aboard the three ships. The men finally recognized Ferdinand Magellan as a great captain and a superb navigator. They were proud to be part of one of the most important voyages of all time.

On March 31, 1521, Magellan and his men celebrated Easter. Success had made Magellan a very religious man. He felt that because God had protected him, he should try to convert the Islanders.

He did convert one chief. But he made a fatal
mistake when he agreed to help the chief in a fight
with an enemy on the nearby island of Mactan.

When Magellan and sixty volunteers landed on
Mactan at midnight on April 27, 1521, they were
surprised to see how greatly the fierce tribesmen
outnumbered them.

Magellan ordered a retreat. Then, when most of
his men had escaped, he was struck by a warrior's
spear!

He was killed at the very moment of his great
success.

The sailors were stunned. How could this brave and determined leader, who had fearlessly faced mutiny, scurvy, storms, and great hardships, be killed in such a needless battle?

By the time the battle was over, many of the officers and crewmen had been killed. Desperate and frightened—without a leader and navigator— they were almost helpless. For weeks, the weather-beaten ships sailed about in the Pacific Ocean, looking for the Spice Islands—only a short distance to the southeast. When they finally arrived there, they took on a load of cloves.

There were not enough men left to sail three ships, so they burned the worm-eaten *Concepción*. A few weeks later, the *Trinidad* was wrecked in a storm. Only the *Victoria* was left to sail on to Spain.

On September 6, 1522, the rotting old *Victoria* arrived in Seville. The first voyage around the world had taken almost three years! Only eighteen men of the original crew were aboard. The pilot, Sebastian del Cano, was in command, and the king honored him as the first man to sail around the world.

But it is to Ferdinand Magellan that history has rightly given the credit for circumnavigating the globe. Few voyages have been so difficult. The determined Portuguese navigator proved without question that the world was round—and that brave people could circle it.